The Art of Good Food

STUFFED VEGETABLES

The Art of Good Food

STUFFED VEGETABLES

JON HIGGINS

Illustrated by

PAUL COLLICUTT

CHARTWELL
BOOKS, INC.

The Art of Good Food

STUFFED VEGETABLES

Designed and created by

THE BRIDGEWATER BOOK COMPANY LTD

Designer Sarah Stanley

Editor Donna Wood

Managing Editor Anna Clarkson

Illustrations Paul Collicutt

Page makeup Heidi Green

CHARTWELL BOOKS

A division of Book Sales, Inc.

POST OFFICE BOX 7100

114 Northfield Avenue

Edison, N.J. 08837

CLB 4591

Color separation by Sussex Repro, England

Printed and bound in Singapore by Tien Wah Press

ISBN 0-7858-0377-7

Contents

*I*ntroduction

Most of us can remember sitting at the dinner table feeling sorry for ourselves and being told: "Eat up all your vegetables, they're good for you," which would later progress to:"If you don't eat them, you won't get any dessert."

Confronted by a plate of uninspiring and often overcooked vegetables that never strayed beyond the safe realm of the more common varieties, is it any wonder that many of us turned away from what was potentially the most exciting and healthiest part of the meal, and have probably carried a mental note to eat only the minimum of vegetables ever since?

However, in recent years there has been increasing evidence that properly cooked vegetables, besides containing lots of essential vitamins, have the ability to help our bodies fight off illness and disease.

Knowing we should increase our vegetable intake is all well and good, but a dim recollection of soggy Brussels sprouts and anemic carrots still deters many people from taking this course. This collection of recipes is designed to rekindle interest in not only the common varieties of vegetable but also some more unusual types that are not often featured in recipe books. From the humble backed potato to the globe artichoke and custard squash there are recipes to cater for many different occasions and to suit a wide variety of tastes.

USEFUL TIPS ON BUYING VEGETABLES

1. If you buy your vegetables from a supermarket or a similar self-service style store don't always pick those at the top of the pile. If the retailer correctly rotates the stock this will correspondingly be the oldest, and while there may be nothing wrong with it on the day of purchase, it will be the first to deteriorate later, an important factor to consider if you do not plan to use the item for a couple of days.

2. A perfect-looking vegetable is not always the one with the most flavor. Be discerning; try several different varieties and decide which you prefer, regardless of which is the most visually perfect.

3. In most supermarkets fruit and vegetables are the first goods to be placed into the shopping cart, and often end up squashed. Try to keep an area in your shopping cart solely for these delicate items.

4. When buying certain vegetables, such as broccoli, by loose weight, remember that you are paying for a length of useless stalk that will just be thrown away!

5. Once you get your vegetables home, remove any cellophane wrappings. If this is not done, condensation will form and the vegetables will deteriorate rapidly.

6. Vegetables last longer stored in a cool, dry place with plenty of ventilation, but of course the sooner you use them the fresher they taste.

7. Any trimmings from fresh vegetables or vegetables slightly past their peak are ideal for making fresh stock. Place them in a saucepan, cover with water and simmer gently for about 30 minutes. If you have no immediate use for the stock, allow it to cool completely before pouring into suitable containers and placing in the freezer.

Homemade Mayonnaise

Several recipes in this book use mayonnaise, and since fresh mayonnaise is so much more delicious than store-bought varieties, I have included a recipe that is simplicity itself.

INGREDIENTS
2 egg yolks
1 tablespoon lemon juice
1 1/4 cups olive oil
1 teaspoon English mustard powder
1/4 teaspoon salt
1/4 teaspoon freshly ground black pepper
1 tablespoon white wine vinegar

Place the egg yolks, lemon juice, salt and mustard powder in a bowl and beat thoroughly for a couple of minutes until all the ingredients are blended together.

Slowly add the olive oil a little at a time, beating well between each addition, until the sauce becomes thick and smooth. This process takes a little time to complete so do not be tempted to rush by adding the oil too quickly because this may cause the mayonnaise to separate.

If separation does occur, place a fresh egg yolk in a mixing bowl and gradually beat the mayonnaise into it. This will correct the consistency.

To finish the mayonnaise stir in the pepper and wine vinegar and chill in the refrigerator until required.

Cabbage Leaves with Chicken & Nut Stuffing

SERVES 6

This hearty recipe will satisfy the most ravenous of appetites

INGREDIENTS
1 large savoy cabbage
8 ounces cooked chicken, finely chopped
4 ounces long grain rice, cooked
4 ounces chopped walnuts
1 egg, beaten
salt and freshly ground black pepper
2 ounces Parmesan cheese, grated

FOR THE SAUCE
1 medium onion, chopped
2 tablespoons olive oil
14-ounce can chopped tomatoes
1 tablespoon tomato paste
4 tablespoons clear honey

Using a sharp knife cut the leaves off the cabbage at the stalk and carefully remove them one at a time. Discard the outermost leaves and rinse the remainder under cold water.

Bring a large saucepan of water to a boil and drop in three or four leaves at a time. Push them under the surface with a slotted spoon and leave until soft and pliable. Remove from the water and allow to drain. Repeat this process until all the leaves are blanched.

Mix together the cooked chicken, rice and chopped walnuts and bind them together with the beaten egg. Season the mixture with plenty of salt and black pepper.

Cut away the very hard stalk at the base of each cabbage leaf and place a tablespoon of stuffing in the center. Roll the cabbage leaf tightly, folding in the sides to create a neat parcel.

Place the stuffed leaves seam-side down in a lightly greased ovenproof dish. Pack the leaves tightly until the dish is full.

To make the sauce, fry the chopped onion in the olive oil until softened and lightly browned. Add the canned tomatoes and tomato paste to the pan and bring to a boil for a few minutes to reduce slightly.

Stir in the honey and season well.

Pour the sauce evenly over the stuffed cabbage and place the dish in a preheated oven at 375°F for approximately 45 minutes.

10 minutes before cooking is complete, sprinkle the Parmesan cheese over the top of the cabbage and return the dish to the oven. The cheese will melt and form a delicious crust. Serve immediately.

TIME: *Preparation takes about 45 minutes.*
Cooking takes approximately 1 hour 15 minutes.

12

Potato & Bacon-stuffed Grape Leaves

SERVES 4

These potato parcels taste great in tomato sauce

INGREDIENTS

1 package grape leaves in brine (approx. 16 leaves)
1 pound new potatoes
salt and freshly ground black pepper
4 tablespoons butter
2 cloves garlic, roughly chopped
8 ounces unsmoked bacon, rind removed
2 tablespoons chopped parsley

FOR THE SAUCE

2 tablespoons olive oil
1 medium onion, finely chopped
2 cloves garlic, finely chopped
14-ounce can chopped tomatoes
1 tablespoon tomato paste
1 tablespoon sugar

▌Remove the grape leaves from their packaging, place them in a shallow bowl and cover with cold water. Set aside for 20 minutes then drain off the water and carefully separate the leaves. Lay them out on paper towel to absorb the excess moisture.

▌Scrub any excess soil from the potatoes and boil them in plenty of salted water until they are slightly undercooked, drain and allow to cool.

▌Melt the butter in a skillet over a low heat. Turn up the heat and fry the garlic until golden brown.

▌Cut the bacon into ½-inch pieces, add to the skillet and fry until crispy and brown.

▌While the bacon is frying cut the potatoes into slices, add to the skillet and toss them regularly until they brown also. Do not worry if the potatoes break up a little.

▌Remove the skillet from the heat and add the chopped parsley and plenty of black pepper.

▌To make the sauce, heat the olive oil in a saucepan and fry the onion and garlic until soft. Add the chopped tomatoes and tomato paste and bring the sauce to a boil. Allow a few minutes for the sauce to reduce. Stir in the sugar, add some seasoning and remove from the heat.

▌Spoon a small amount of the potato mixture into the center of a grape leaf and roll it up, folding in the sides to produce a neat, square parcel. Repeat the process with the other grape leaves and arrange them in a lightly greased ovenproof dish.

▌If there is any potato mixture left, spread it over the stuffed grape leaves and pour the tomato sauce over, ensuring it gets between them.

▌Cover tightly with tinfoil and place in a preheated oven at 375°F for 45 minutes. Serve immediately.

TIME: *Preparation takes about 30 minutes. Cooking takes approximately 1 hour 15 minutes.*

14

Roasted Peppers with Bacon & Pasta

SERVES 4

The combination of pepper and pasta is very Italian

INGREDIENTS

2 large red bell peppers
2 large yellow bell peppers
olive oil
6 ounces farfalle
6 slices smoked bacon
1 tablespoon green pesto
1 tablespoon fresh basil, chopped
2 tablespoons Parmesan cheese, grated
salt and freshly ground black pepper

Cut the peppers in half lengthways and deseed. Brush with a little olive oil and lay them on a baking sheet.

Place in a preheated oven at 375°F until the peppers soften and the skins begin to blister and char. This will take approximately 15 minutes.

While the peppers are cooking, bring a large saucepan of salted water to a boil. Add a few drops of oil to the pan to prevent sticking and throw in the pasta. Cook the pasta until just tender (al dente).

Place the bacon slices on a wire rack under a preheated broiler and cook until very dry and crispy. Remove and crumble them between the fingers.

Drain the cooked pasta thoroughly and tip it into a bowl, stir in the bacon, pesto, Parmesan, chopped basil and lots of pepper.

The peppers should now be roasted to perfection. Remove them from the oven and carefully transfer them to their serving dishes.

Pile spoonfuls of the pasta mixture into each pepper half and drizzle over a little extra olive oil.

Serve immediately with lots of crusty bread to mop up the excess oil.

TIME: *Preparation takes about 10 minutes. Cooking takes approximately 20 minutes.*

18

Stuffed Cucumber in White Wine Sauce

SERVES 4

You can use cucumber for so much more than just salads

INGREDIENTS

1 large or 2 medium cucumbers

2 tablespoons olive oil

1 medium onion, finely chopped

6 ounces mushrooms, finely chopped

4 ounces thin sliced ham, finely chopped

1 teaspoon dried cilantro

6 tablespoons white wine

²/₃ cup light cream

1 tablespoon fresh parsley, chopped

olive oil

salt and freshly ground black pepper

Wipe the cucumber, remove the ends and cut into 4 equal lengths. Cut each piece in half and remove the seeds using a teaspoon. Set to one side.

To prepare the stuffing, heat the olive oil in a skillet and fry the onion until soft, do not allow it to color. Add the chopped mushrooms to the skillet and stir into the onion; continue frying until the mushrooms have absorbed some of the skillet juices and become darker in color.

Add the ham and dried cilantro to the skillet and stir into the stuffing with plenty of seasoning.

Arrange the prepared cucumber in a lightly greased ovenproof dish and place spoonfuls of the stuffing into the hollowed out centers. Spread any remaining stuffing over the top.

Drizzle over a little olive oil and lightly season with salt and pepper.

Place in a preheated oven at 350°F for approximately 20 minutes or until the cucumber is tender.

Just before the cooking time is complete, reheat the skillet for a few seconds and pour in the wine. This will lift any of the stuffing still left in the skillet and add flavor to the sauce.

Reduce the wine briefly and remove the skillet from the heat. Stir in the cream and add the chopped parsley and a little seasoning.

Arrange the stuffed cucumber in a serving dish and spoon a little of the sauce over each piece. Serve immediately.

TIME: *Preparation takes about 20 minutes. Cooking takes approximately 45 minutes.*

Eggplant with Kabanos

SERVES 4

This Polish pork sausage is now widely available

INGREDIENTS
2 medium eggplants
salt and freshly ground black pepper
2 cloves garlic, thinly sliced
2 medium onions, thinly sliced
8 Kabanos sausages
8 ounces large flat mushrooms, thinly sliced
2 tablespoons parsley, finely chopped
4 tablespoons fresh breadcrumbs
4 tablespoons olive oil

Cut the eggplants in half lengthways and sprinkle with salt. Leave them for approximately 30 minutes to extract the juices, then wash off the salt and pat dry with paper towel.

Make deep cuts into the flesh of the eggplant halves and place them in an ovenproof dish, sprinkle generously with water and cover tightly with tinfoil.

Place in a preheated oven at 350°F for approximately 45 minutes or until the flesh has softened. Keep a watchful eye on them because you do not want them to overcook and lose their shape.

While they are cooking prepare the filling. Fry the onion and garlic in 2 tablespoons of olive oil until they are golden brown. Spoon them onto paper towel and set aside.

Remove the skin from the kabanos and cut them into $1/2$-inch chunks. Heat the remaining olive oil and fry briefly until lightly browned.

Add the mushrooms to the skillet. Toss them among the sausages so they absorb the olive oil and cooking juices. Return the cooked onion and garlic to the pan and briefly fry the whole lot together. Season generously with plenty of salt and pepper.

When the eggplants are cooked, scoop out the flesh leaving a good $1/2$-inch thickness next to the skin. Chop half of the removed flesh and stir it into the filling.

Pile the filling into the eggplant shells and arrange them on a baking sheet.

Mix together the chopped parsley, breadcrumbs and a few twists of black pepper and sprinkle the mixture generously over the stuffed eggplants. Drizzle a small amount of olive oil over the top of each one.

Place them in the oven for 20 minutes to heat through thoroughly and serve immediately.

TIME: *Preparation takes about 25 minutes, plus standing.*
Cooking takes approximately 1 hour.

21

Stuffed Custard Squash

SERVES 4

Custard squashes are available during summer and should be used when very ripe

INGREDIENTS
1 ripe custard squash
1 large onion, chopped
2 cloves garlic, chopped
2 tablespoons olive oil
12 ounces lean ground beef
1 tablespoon tomato paste
14-ounce can chopped tomatoes
14-ounce can red kidney beans, drained
salt and freshly ground black pepper
3 tablespoons Red Leicester cheese, grated

‖ Cut the top from the squash and remove all the seeds using a spoon. Set to one side. Preheat the oven to 375°F.

‖ Heat the olive oil in a saucepan and cook the onion and garlic until soft and nicely browned. Add the ground beef to the pan and cook until sealed and just beginning to brown.

‖ Stir in the tomato paste, chopped tomatoes and kidney beans and season generously with salt and black pepper. Bring the pan to a boil, then reduce the heat and allow to simmer, stirring occasionally, for approximately 30 minutes until the meat is tender. If the sauce begins to look a little dry at any stage during cooking add a little cold water.

‖ When the meat sauce is cooked, spoon it into the squash and sprinkle over the grated cheese.

‖ Place the stuffed squash on a baking sheet and place in the oven for 30 minutes. Keep an eye on it while it is cooking; custard squash is a thin-skinned vegetable with tender flesh, so you may find the cooking time can be reduced depending on its ripeness.

‖ Place the cooked squash on a large serving platter. Serve with plenty of salt and pepper and some extra cheese for sprinkling.

TIME: *Preparation takes about 20 minutes. Cooking takes approximately 1 hour 10 minutes.*

22

Stuffed Zucchinis in Cheese Sauce

SERVES 4

The humble zucchini has never tasted this good

INGREDIENTS

4 large zucchinis

2 tablespoons olive oil

1 small onion, finely chopped

2 cloves garlic, crushed

1 carrot, roughly chopped

4 ounces rindless bacon, chopped

8 ounces fresh ground beef

2 tablespoons tomato paste

$^2/_3$ cup red wine

$^2/_3$ cup beef stock

salt and freshly ground black pepper

FOR THE CHEESE SAUCE

1 tablespoon butter

1 tablespoon flour

$1^1/_4$ cups fresh milk

4 ounces Cheddar cheese, grated

Bring a large saucepan of water to a boil and drop in the zucchinis to blanch for 10 minutes.

Remove the blanched zucchinis from the water and cut them in half lengthways. Use a teaspoon to remove some of the flesh from the centers. Arrange them in a lightly greased ovenproof dish. Set aside.

Heat the olive oil in a saucepan and fry the onion and garlic until softened and lightly browned. Add the carrot and bacon and continue frying until the bacon is cooked.

Add the ground beef to the pan and fry briefly until the meat is sealed. Stir in the tomato paste and continue frying for a couple of minutes.

Pour in the wine and beef stock and season well. Reduce the heat, and simmer for 30 minutes, stirring occasionally, until tender and reduced in quantity.

Melt the butter in a saucepan and stir in the flour. Cook briefly for a minute or two then slowly stir in the milk until you have a smooth sauce. Add half the grated cheese to the sauce and season well.

Spoon the meat into the hollowed-out zucchinis and pour any remaining over the top. Cover with the cheese sauce and sprinkle the remaining grated cheese over the top.

Finish with a few twists of fresh pepper and place in a preheated oven at 350°F for 30 minutes until the dish is well heated through and the cheese has melted to a lovely crust.

Serve immediately with a crisp green salad.

TIME: *Preparation takes about 20 minutes.*
Cooking takes approximately 1 hour 30 minutes.

24

Stuffed Fennel

SERVES 4

This is a great way to enjoy the unique flavor of fennel

INGREDIENTS

4 large fennel bulbs

2 tablespoons olive oil

1 small onion, finely chopped

2 cloves garlic, finely chopped

8 ounces lean ground beef

1 tablespoon tomato paste

1 tablespoon medium hot chili sauce

fresh breadcrumbs

salt and freshly ground black pepper

Cut the stalks from the top of the fennel and place the bulbs in a steamer. Steam for about 30 minutes or until they begin to soften. Do not overcook or they will fall apart.

While the fennel is cooking prepare the meat stuffing. Heat the olive oil in a skillet and fry the onion and garlic until they have softened and browned a little.

Add the ground beef to the skillet and fry it until it is sealed and beginning to brown. Add the tomato paste and chili sauce along with sufficient cold water to moisten.

Season the sauce well and allow to simmer for about 30 minutes, adding a little more water as and when necessary to prevent it from drying out.

When the fennel has finished steaming, carefully ease open the outer leaves, and using a sharp knife, make cuts into the inside of the fennel. Using a teaspoon, scoop out the insides leaving a good thickness of "shell."

Roughly chop the fennel insides and stir them into the meat sauce.

Arrange the fennel bulbs in a lightly greased ovenproof dish and spoon the meat sauce into them. Spoon any remaining sauce over the top of the bulbs, and sprinkle thickly with breadcrumbs.

Season the finished dish with plenty of black pepper and place in a preheated oven at 350°F for 15–20 minutes until well heated through. Serve immediately.

TIME: *Preparation takes about 20 minutes. Cooking takes approximately 1 hour.*

Whole Stuffed Cabbage

SERVES 6

Amaze your fellow diners with this impressive-looking dish

INGREDIENTS
1 savoy cabbage
1 small onion, finely chopped
1 pound best-quality sausagemeat
1 tablespoon tomato paste
salt and freshly ground black pepper

Discard any rough-looking leaves from the cabbage so you are left with the tightly packed heart.

With a sharp knife cut the top from the cabbage and carefully remove the insides leaving a "wall" about 1 inch thick all the way around.

Bring a large saucepan of water to a boil and blanch the cabbage shell and top for 5 minutes until it just begins to soften. Drain thoroughly.

Using your hands, mix together the chopped onion, sausagemeat and tomato paste and season well. Stuff the inside of the cabbage with the sausagemeat mix and use a few leaves from the top of the cabbage to cover.

Tie the cabbage in a double thickness of cheesecloth and place in a pan of boiling water for an hour.

When cooked, carefully remove the cabbage from the saucepan and drain thoroughly. Remove the cheesecloth and place the whole cabbage on a serving dish. Cut the stuffed cabbage into 6 portions at the table.

TIME: *Preparation takes about 20 minutes.*
Cooking takes approximately 1 hour.

26

Radishes with Pâté

MAKES APPROXIMATELY 30

These make great little "pop-in-the-mouth" appetizers to serve before a meal

INGREDIENTS
1 bunch of large radishes
4 ounces pâté de foie gras (or similar)
4 tablespoons butter
salt and freshly ground black pepper
poppy seeds (for decoration)

This recipe successfully combines the radish, much used as an hors-d'oeuvre in Lebanese cooking, with the very French pâté de foie gras.

Cut the stalks and roots from the radishes to provide a flat surface to stand on. Wash the trimmed radishes under cold running water and cut them in half widthways.

Using a melon baller, remove a portion of the white center of the radish and discard. Keep the radishes in a bowl of cold water until you fill them.

In a separate bowl, pound together the butter and pâté with a little seasoning until they are well mixed and nicely softened. Spoon the mixture into a small piping bag with a decorative nozzle.

Drain the radish halves and dry on paper towel, then pipe in a rosette of the pâté mixture so that it stands just proud of the top of the radish.

When all the radish halves are stuffed, stand them close together on their serving dish and sprinkle liberally with poppy seeds. Keep refrigerated before serving.

TIME: *Preparation takes about 20 minutes.*

Lebanese-style Zucchinis

SERVES 4

These stuffed zucchinis are a meal in themselves

INGREDIENTS
2 tablespoons olive oil
1 small onion, finely chopped
2 cloves garlic, crushed
4 ounces brown rice, washed
2 ounces pine nuts
12 ounces ground lamb
pinch of cinnamon, ground cloves and ground chili
freshly ground black pepper
6 medium zucchinis
1¼ cups red wine
1¼ cups beef stock
cornstarch to thicken the sauce

Heat the olive oil and gently fry the onion and garlic until soft. Stir in the washed rice and pine nuts and fry briefly to coat them with oil.

Remove the pan from the heat and spoon the mixture into a food processor. Briefly process until the mixture is coarsely chopped.

Pound the ground lamb and spices in a pestle and mortar until smooth then place in a mixing bowl along with the rice mixture.

Using your hands, mix the two together thoroughly and season with plenty of black pepper.

Slice the ends from the zucchinis and carefully remove as much of the flesh as possible, leaving a thin layer next to the skin, using an apple corer.

Pack each zucchini as full as possible with the stuffing mix and place them side-by-side in a shallow, lightly greased ovenproof dish.

Pour over the red wine and beef stock, cover and place in a preheated oven at 375°F for approximately 30 minutes or until the zucchinis are tender.

When cooked, remove the stuffed zucchinis from the oven, arrange on a serving dish and keep hot.

Thicken the cooking liquor with a little cornstarch dissolved in water and spoon over the zucchinis. Serve immediately.

TIME: *Preparation takes about 30 minutes. Cooking takes approximately 30 minutes.*

28

Couscous Red Cabbage

SERVES 4

Red cabbage and couscous make an excellent partnership

INGREDIENTS

1 red cabbage

8 ounces couscous

6 ounces cooked lamb, shredded

4 ounces dried apricots, finely chopped

2$\frac{1}{2}$ cups vegetable stock

salt and freshly ground black pepper

Remove the rough outer leaves from the cabbage until you are left with the tightly packed heart. Carefully remove the leaves one at a time taking care not to damage them.

Bring a large saucepan of water to a boil and drop in the cabbage leaves for a few minutes to soften them sufficiently so they can be rolled. Blanch a few at a time so that you do not overcook them.

Remove the cabbage leaves from the water and lay them on paper towel to soak up any excess moisture. Use a sharp knife to cut away the hard stalk at the base of the leaves.

Spread out the couscous in a heatproof dish and cover with boiling water. Set to one side for 15–20 minutes until the couscous has absorbed the water and is ready to use.

Stir the lamb and dried apricots into the couscous and season well.

Spoon some couscous stuffing mixture onto the middle of the cabbage leaves and roll them up, folding the sides in as you roll. Place the stuffed leaves seam-side down in a lightly greased ovenproof dish.

When the dish is full, pour over sufficient stock to cover the base of the dish and cover with tinfoil. Bake in a preheated oven at 350°F for 30 minutes or until the cabbage leaves are tender.

Carefully remove the leaves from the stock with a slotted spoon and arrange on a serving dish.

TIME: *Preparation takes about 25 minutes. Cooking takes approximately 1 hour.*

29

Stuffed Grape Leaves

SERVES 4

These are a great favorite of the Russians but are equally popular here

INGREDIENTS

1 package grape leaves in brine (approx. 16 leaves)

1 tablespoon olive oil

2 shallots, finely chopped

6 ounces ground lamb

1 teaspoon hot chili sauce

2 ounces wild rice, cooked

1 ounce raisins

1 ounce pine nuts

2 tablespoons chopped fresh mint

salt and freshly ground black pepper

1¼ cups chicken stock

Greek yogurt, to serve (optional)

Remove the grape leaves from their packaging, place in a shallow bowl and cover with cold water. Set aside for 20 minutes then drain off the water and carefully separate the leaves. Lay them out on paper towel to absorb the excess moisture.

Heat the olive oil in a skillet and briefly fry the chopped shallots until softened. Add the ground lamb and continue to cook until the meat is sealed and just beginning to brown. Add the chili sauce.

Stir in the wild rice, raisins, pine nuts and chopped fresh mint and season well.

Place a tablespoon of the lamb mixture in the center of a grape leaf, fold in the sides and roll up to form a neat, tight parcel.

Repeat this process with the remaining grape leaves and pack them into the bottom of a saucepan. If the saucepan is not big enough cover the first layer with a couple of spare grape leaves and begin a second.

When all the grape leaves are stuffed, pour over the chicken stock, cover with a lid and place over a low heat to simmer for approximately 45 minutes.

When cooked, carefully remove the stuffed leaves from the stock with a slotted spoon and arrange on a serving dish. Alternatively, leave to cool and serve with Greek yogurt flavored with a little chopped mint.

TIME: *Preparation takes about 30 minutes. Cooking takes approximately 50 minutes.*

Radicchio Leaves with Coconut Chicken

MAKES 12

The *bitter radicchio leaves taste wonderful with the sweet chicken*

INGREDIENTS

1 whole fresh coconut

2 ripe bananas

juice of 2 limes

12 ounces cooked chicken breast

2 tablespoons olive oil

12 radicchio leaves

1 ounce slivered almonds, toasted

Drill two small holes at one end of the coconut and drain off the milk, then give the shell a sharp tap with a hammer to get to the flesh.

Peel and chop the bananas into ³/₄-inch chunks, and roll them in a little of the lime juice to prevent them from discoloring.

Cut the chicken into similar sized pieces and mix these with the banana chunks.

Put the remaining lime juice, olive oil, 2 tablespoons of coconut milk and 1 tablespoon grated coconut in a screw-top jar with a tight-fitting lid and shake thoroughly to mix.

Pour the marinade over the chicken and banana and stir. Cover and leave to marinate for at least an hour.

When the chicken has marinated, carefully remove it from the liquid using a slotted spoon and divide it equally among the radicchio leaves.

Sprinkle a few lightly toasted almond slivers over the top of each leaf and roll them up; secure each roll with a wooden toothpick and arrange on a serving dish. Keep refrigerated before serving.

TIME: *Preparation takes about 25 minutes, plus marinating.*

31

Wild Rice Boats

SERVES 4

These not only taste great, but look attractive when served

INGREDIENTS

2 medium eggplants

salt and freshly ground black pepper

6 ounces wild rice, washed

chicken stock

8 slices unsmoked bacon

olive oil

2 ounces black olives, pitted and sliced

2 ounces frozen peas, defrosted

butter

Cut the eggplants in half lengthways, sprinkle the cut surface with plenty of salt and leave to stand for 30 minutes. Wash off the salt and extracted juices and dry with paper towel.

Score the eggplant flesh with a sharp knife, but do not pierce the skin. Place the eggplants in an ovenproof dish with a sprinkling of water. Cover and cook in a medium oven at 350°F until the flesh is soft. Take care not to overcook the eggplants because they may collapse.

While they are cooking, put the rice in a saucepan with sufficient chicken stock to just cover it. Do not add any salt because the stock will be sufficiently salty. Place the pan on the heat and bring to a boil, reduce to a simmer and cook the rice until most of the stock has been absorbed and the grains are still slightly firm. Strain to remove any excess liquid and set to one side.

Chop the bacon into $1/2$-inch lengths and fry it in a little olive oil until nicely browned and crispy.

Put the cooked rice, bacon, sliced olives and peas in a mixing bowl and stir together with plenty of black pepper.

Scoop out the eggplant flesh leaving a thin layer next to the skin, roughly chop and add to the rice mixture.

Generously fill the skins with the rice mixture and put a small knob of butter on top of each.

Place the stuffed eggplant skins on a baking sheet and return them to the oven for 15–20 minutes until heated through. Serve immediately.

TIME: *Preparation takes about 15 minutes, plus standing.*
Cooking takes approximately 45 minutes.

33

$\mathcal{L}$azy $\mathcal{S}$hrimp

SERVES 4

A *recipe to make you yearn for those hot summer days*

INGREDIENTS
18 cooked shrimp, shelled
2 large heads of endive
chicory and radicchio leaves
1 lemon, sliced
4 cooked shrimp, unshelled, for decoration
(optional)

FOR THE MARINADE
4 tablespoons virgin olive oil
juice of 1 lemon
salt and freshly ground black pepper
1 tablespoon balsamic vinegar

▌Place all the ingredients for the marinade into a screw-top jar and shake well to mix.

▌Place the shrimp in a shallow dish and pour the marinade over, gently tossing the shrimp to coat them evenly. Cover and refrigerate for a couple of hours.

▌Discard any damaged outer leaves from the endive and gently break off the inner leaves. Rinse them under cold running water and pat dry with paper towel.

▌Wash sufficient chicory and radicchio lettuce to completely cover a large oval meat platter, drain thoroughly and arrange attractively.

▌Remove the shrimp from the marinade and lay one shrimp on each piece of endive. Arrange these on the bed of lettuce.

▌Pour any remaining marinade over the lettuce and garnish with the lemon slices and cooked unshelled shrimp, if using. Serve with chunks of fresh bread and plenty of chilled white wine.

TIME: *Preparation takes about 25 minutes, plus marinating.*

34

Avocado Soufflé

SERVES 4

A *lighter way to enjoy avocados*

INGREDIENTS
2 ripe avocados
2 ounces cooked shelled shrimp, mashed
1 tablespoon butter
1 tablespoon flour
²/₃ cup fresh milk
salt and freshly ground black pepper
2 eggs, separated

Cut the avocados in half lengthways and gently separate the two halves, remove the stone and discard.

Using a teaspoon, carefully scoop out all the flesh from the avocados into a bowl, taking care not to damage the skins. Mash the avocado flesh to a fine paste and beat together with the mashed shrimp, then set to one side with the skins.

Over a gentle heat melt the butter in a saucepan, add the flour and stir the two together for a few minutes to allow the flour to cook.

Slowly add the milk, a few drops at a time to begin with, then increase the flow until all the milk has been added and the sauce is thick and smooth. Remove the pan from the heat and season with a good pinch of salt and lots of freshly ground black pepper.

Beat together the mashed avocado, the sauce and the egg yolks until the mixture is smooth.

In a clean bowl whisk the egg whites until they form stiff peaks and fold them into the avocado mixture. Spoon the mixture into the 4 avocado skins and place them on a baking sheet.

Bake them in a preheated oven at 400°F for approximately 20 minutes or until they are well risen and golden brown. Serve immediately.

TIME: *Preparation takes about 20 minutes. Cooking takes approximately 35 minutes.*

Sardine-stuffed Onions

SERVES 4

Onions taste wonderful when roasted in the oven

INGREDIENTS

2 large onions
8-ounce can sardines in tomato sauce
salt and freshly ground black pepper
2 ounces long grain rice, cooked
2 ounces raisins
fresh breadcrumbs
olive oil

Do not peel the onions. Place them directly onto the shelf of a preheated oven at 400°F for 30 minutes.

Remove the sardines from the can and mash them lightly with plenty of seasoning. Stir in the cooked rice and raisins.

When the onions have had 30 minutes cooking time remove from the oven and peel them. Cut them in half from top to bottom and remove some of the layers from the middle to create an onion bowl.

Fill the hollowed out onions with the sardine stuffing and place them on a baking sheet. Sprinkle generously with the fresh breadcrumbs and drizzle with a little olive oil. Reduce the oven temperature to 350°F and return the stuffed onions to cook for a further 20 minutes.

Serve immediately, either as a starter or with potatoes and vegetables as a main course.

TIME: *Preparation takes about 30 minutes. Cooking takes approximately 50 minutes.*

37

Beef Tomato Niçoise

SERVES 4

This is based on a traditional salad recipe but served inside a tomato shell

INGREDIENTS

4 beef tomatoes, evenly sized

2 ounces pitted black olives, halved

2 hard boiled eggs, roughly chopped

2 red baby bell peppers, seeded and sliced

1 tablespoon salted peanuts

handful of rocket leaves, roughly torn

8 anchovy fillets

fresh lettuce leaves, to serve

FOR THE DRESSING

4 tablespoons white wine vinegar

1 teaspoon Dijon mustard

6 tablespoons best-quality olive oil

salt and freshly ground black pepper

Wash the beef tomatoes under cold running water and dry using a dish towel.

Slice the tops off the tomatoes and carefully remove the insides using a teaspoon. Discard.

Place the black olives, chopped eggs, sliced peppers, peanuts and rocket in a mixing bowl and gently toss together using your hands.

Place all the ingredients for the dressing in a clean screw-top jar and shake vigorously to combine. Try a little on a teaspoon first to check the taste is to your liking before pouring a small quantity onto the salad and lightly tossing. Do not feel obliged to use all the dressing; it can be refrigerated for future use.

Spoon the dressed salad into the tomato skins, brush the outside of the tomatoes with a little of the dressing to give a shine and finish each tomato with 2 anchovy fillets laid over the top in a cross.

Serve on a bed of fresh lettuce leaves with lots of crusty bread and a twist of black pepper.

TIME: *Preparation takes about 30 minutes.*

Zucchinis with Mackerel & Herbs

SERVES 4

This makes a great healthy snack

INGREDIENTS
2 medium zucchinis
4 smoked mackerel fillets, cooked and skinned
2 eggs, beaten
2 tablespoons olive oil
1 tablespoon fresh chopped fennel leaves
1 tablespoon fresh tarragon, chopped
2 ounces red Leicester cheese, grated
salt and freshly ground black pepper

▌ Cut the zucchinis in half lengthways and carefully remove the insides using a teaspoon, leaving a thin layer of flesh next to the skin.
▌ Break the smoked mackerel into small pieces and place in a mixing bowl. Moisten the fish with the beaten egg and, using a fork, mash it to a paste.
▌ Chop the zucchini insides and fry in the olive oil for 5 minutes until they soften. Add to the fish.
▌ Beat the chopped fennel leaves, tarragon and grated cheese into the mackerel mixture and season well.
▌ Spoon the stuffing into the zucchini skins and place in a lightly greased ovenproof dish. Cook in a preheated oven at 375°F for 20 minutes.
▌ Serve immediately with a small green salad.

TIME: *Preparation takes about 20 minutes.*
Cooking takes approximately 25 minutes.

Smoked Salmon & Lettuce Rolls

SERVES 4

This is an excellent way of serving smoked salmon without the need for cutlery

INGREDIENTS
1 oak leaf lettuce
12 slices smoked salmon
freshly ground black pepper
lemon juice
lemon wedges, to garnish

▌ Remove the rough outer leaves from the lettuce and carefully pick the 12 choicest leaves from those remaining. Wash in a little cold water and shake to remove the excess moisture. Be gentle with the lettuce leaves during this process because you want them to remain as full of life as possible.
▌ Place a slice of smoked salmon on each leaf, season with plenty of black pepper and sprinkle with a little lemon juice.
▌ Roll the leaf quite tightly in a fan shape and place on a serving dish with the end of the leaf underneath.
▌ Repeat this process with the remaining leaves and pack them tightly together. Garnish with lemon wedges and serve.

TIME: *Preparation takes about 20 minutes.*

Warm Avocado with Creole Shrimp

SERVES 4

Hot avocado tastes great with these fruity shrimp

INGREDIENTS
2 large ripe avocados
1 lime
2 tablespoons olive oil
1/2 bunch scallions, finely chopped
2 cloves garlic, chopped
2 tomatoes, skinned and chopped
1 red bell pepper, seeded and chopped
1 tablespoon tomato paste
few drops of Tabasco
12 ounces large cooked shelled shrimp
freshly ground black pepper
lime wedges, to garnish

Cut the avocados in half lengthways and gently separate the 2 halves. Remove the stone and discard.

Cut the lime in half and rub it over the cut surface of the avocado. Arrange the avocados in an ovenproof dish and place in a preheated oven at 350°F for 10–15 minutes. It is important that the flesh just heats through and does not overcook.

While the avocado is cooking heat the oil in a wok or saucepan and fry the chopped scallions and garlic for 2 minutes. Add the skinned tomatoes and red pepper and continue frying for a further 2 minutes.

Remove the wok or pan from the heat and stir the tomato paste and a few drops of Tabasco into the vegetables.

Lower the heat. Drain off any liquid from the shrimp, return the pan to the heat, fry the shrimp briefly for 1 minute.

Squeeze the halves of lime and strain the juice to remove the pits. Add the lime juice to the pan along with a few twists of black pepper.

Remove the warmed avocados from the oven and transfer them to serving dishes. Spoon some of the Creole shrimp into the center of each and serve immediately with lime wedges.

TIME: *Preparation takes about 25 minutes. Cooking takes approximately 15 minutes.*

42

Eggplant-wrapped Sardines

SERVES 4

The cooking juices from the fish are absorbed into the eggplant so no flavor is lost

INGREDIENTS
2 medium eggplants
salt and freshly ground black pepper
8 fresh sardines, trimmed, cleaned and descaled
olive oil
4 tablespoons passata or tomato sauce
pitted black olives
tomato or horseradish sauce, to serve

Cut four ½-inch slices from each eggplant, sprinkle them with salt and allow to stand for 30 minutes to extract the bitter juices.

Rinse off the eggplant slices and pat them dry with paper towel. Set to one side.

Wash the sardines under cold running water and dry thoroughly. Arrange on a tinfoil-covered broiler pan, brush with a little olive oil and season well.

Place under a preheated broiler and cook briefly for 3 minutes. Turn the fish, brush over some more olive oil and broil again for 3 minutes.

While the sardines are cooking fry each slice of eggplant in 2 tablespoons of olive oil briefly on each side until it softens and browns a little. Remove from the skillet, spread a little passata over the eggplant and place a sardine widthways across the slice.

Carefully fold the eggplant end to end and pin with half a wooden toothpick. Stud the end of the toothpick with an olive and lay the finished items on a lightly oiled baking sheet.

Place the wrapped sardines in a preheated oven at 350°F for 5 minutes then serve immediately, accompanied by a tomato or horseradish sauce.

TIME: *Preparation takes about 30 minutes, plus standing.*

Cooking takes approximately 30 minutes.

45

$\mathcal{M}$ixed $\mathcal{F}$ish $\mathcal{R}$isotto $\mathcal{P}$eppers

SERVES 4

$\mathcal{C}$reamy risotto and seafood in a crisply roasted red bell pepper

INGREDIENTS

4 large squat red bell peppers

2 tablespoons olive oil

1 small onion, finely chopped

12 ounces risotto rice

5 cups chicken stock

1-pound package, cooked mixed seafood, thawed

salt and freshly ground black pepper

Cut the tops from the peppers and carefully remove the seeds and core. Place the peppers and tops in a large bowl and pour over sufficient boiling water to cover them.

Leave to stand for 5 minutes then pour off the water and leave the peppers upside-down on paper towel to drain thoroughly.

Heat the olive oil in a saucepan and gently fry the chopped onion until soft, but not colored. Add the rice to the pan and fry for a couple of minutes, tossing with the onion so it becomes thoroughly coated in the oil.

Have the stock simmering close to hand. Pour a ladleful of the hot stock onto the rice and stir until it has been absorbed. Stir the rice constantly while it cooks.

Continue this process of adding the stock a ladleful at a time until the risotto becomes thick and creamy but the rice still has a firmness when bitten. This will take about 20–25 minutes.

When the risotto has finished cooking, drain the thawed seafood and stir it into the rice. Season well.

Place the blanched peppers on a baking sheet and spoon in the risotto until just below the rim of the peppers. Place the lids on top, brush the outsides with a little oil and grind over some black pepper.

Place in a preheated oven at 325°F for 35–40 minutes until the pepper is tender. Serve immediately.

TIME: *Preparation takes about 15 minutes. Cooking takes approximately 1 hour 10 minutes.*

Avocado Marie Rose

SERVES *4*

A *deservedly popular dish*

INGREDIENTS
2 firm, ripe avocado pears
washed lettuce leaves
1 quantity mayonnaise (see page 11)
1 tablespoon tomato paste
dash of Tabasco
freshly ground black pepper
12 ounces cooked shelled shrimp, defrosted if frozen
lemon wedges, to garnish

Cut the avocados in half lengthways, gently ease the 2 halves apart and remove the stone. Line 4 small bowls with a few washed lettuce leaves and put an avocado half in each one.
Put the mayonnaise into a bowl and beat in the tomato paste and Tabasco. Season well.
Gently toss the shrimp in the mayonnaise and divide the mixture among the avocados. Do not worry if the mayonnaise runs over the side of the avocado because this adds to the look of the dish.
Garnish with lemon wedges. Serve with thin slices of brown bread and butter and more black pepper.

TIME: *Preparation takes about 15 minutes.*

Chick Pea & Tuna Salad

SERVES *4*

This *delightful salad shows that watching your weight does not have to be boring*

INGREDIENTS
4 iceberg lettuce leaves
1 can chick peas, drained
1 large can tuna chunks in brine
1 bunch scallions, roughly chopped
1 ounce raisins
1 quantity mayonnaise (see page 11)
salt and freshly ground black pepper
mint leaves, to garnish (optional)

Place an iceberg lettuce leaf on each serving plate. There is no need to wash them because the leaves are so tightly packed together there is little chance of soil getting between them.
In a mixing bowl combine the salad ingredients and bind the whole lot together with the mayonnaise.
Season well and spoon the salad into the lettuce leaves. Garnish with a few torn mint leaves if desired and serve right away.

TIME: *Preparation takes about 15 minutes.*

Avocado with Crab & Lime Mayonnaise

SERVES 4

Rich crab meat tastes great mixed with a refreshing homemade mayonnaise

INGREDIENTS
2 firm, ripe avocados
lemon or lime juice
8 ounces white crab meat

FOR THE MAYONNAISE
2 egg yolks
1 teaspoon Dijon mustard
1¼ cups olive oil
grated rind of 1 lime
2 tablespoons lime juice
pinch of salt and freshly ground black pepper
toasted slivered almonds for decoration

Cut the avocados in half lengthways and gently ease the 2 halves apart. Carefully remove the stones. If you are preparing the avocados well in advance of eating, rub the cut surface with a little lemon or lime juice to prevent the flesh from discoloring.

Divide the crab meat into 4 and pile it into the avocado halves. Set to one side while you prepare the mayonnaise.

Place the egg yolks and Dijon mustard in a mixing bowl and beat vigorously until well blended. Begin beating the olive oil into the mixture very slowly, a few drops at a time. Gradually the mayonnaise will begin to thicken, at this point you can increase the flow of olive oil until it is all incorporated and you have a thick, glossy mayonnaise with a lovely pale yellow coloring.

Finish by beating in the grated lime zest juice and season well.

Spoon a generous quantity of the mayonnaise over each avocado half and sprinkle a handful of toasted almonds over. Serve with slices of brown bread and butter and the pepper mill.

TIME: *Preparation takes about 25 minutes.*

Red & White Cabbage Parcels in Vinaigrette

SERVES 4

These stuffed leaves can be prepared well in advance

INGREDIENTS

8 red cabbage leaves

8 savoy cabbage leaves

4 ounces long grain rice, slightly undercooked

1 ounce raisins

4 ounces cooked shelled shrimp

1 tablespoon tomato paste

salt and freshly ground black pepper

FOR THE VINAIGRETTE

2 tablespoons red wine vinegar

4 tablespoons olive oil

salt and freshly ground black pepper

Bring a saucepan of water to a boil and blanch the cabbage leaves 1 or 2 at a time until they are pliable enough to roll up but are not overcooked.

Once blanched, remove the cabbage leaves from the water and lay them out on paper towel to drain thoroughly.

In a large bowl mix together the cooked rice, raisins and shelled shrimp and bind them all together with the tomato paste. Season well.

Cut away any hard stalk from the base of the cabbage leaves and place a spoonful of the filling in the center of each one. Roll them up, folding the sides in as you go to form a neat parcel.

Place the parcels in a steamer, seam-side down, and cook for about 30 minutes until the cabbage leaves are tender. Carefully remove them from the steamer and allow to cool completely.

Place all the ingredients for the vinaigrette in a screw-top jar and shake vigorously to combine thoroughly.

Arrange the stuffed cabbage on a serving dish, mixing the colored leaves together. Pour over the vinaigrette. Allow to stand for a few minutes before serving.

TIME: *Preparation takes about 15 minutes, plus standing.*

Cooking takes approximately 1 hour.

51

Minty Cucumber Pieces

MAKES APPROXIMATELY 24 PIECES

Both mint and cucumber have a very clean taste so they work well together

INGREDIENTS
1 large cucumber
lots of fresh mint leaves
1 tablespoon sugar
4 tablespoons olive oil
4 tablespoons white wine vinegar
salt and freshly ground black pepper
4 ounces soft cream cheese

52

 Using a potato peeler, remove strips of skin from the full length of the cucumber so you are left with an alternating pattern of peeled and unpeeled.

 Cut the cucumber in half lengthways and, using a teaspoon, carefully remove the seeds from the center of both halves. Cut each half into roughly 1-inch chunks and place in a bowl.

 Take a good handful of fresh mint leaves, rinse under cold running water and drain thoroughly. Sprinkle the sugar over and chop very finely.

 Place the chopped mint in a screw-topped jar along with the olive oil, white wine vinegar and seasoning. Shake well to mix the ingredients.

 Pour the marinade over the prepared cucumber, cover and refrigerate for a couple of hours.

 Wash and finely chop another handful of mint leaves and beat into the cream cheese along with a little seasoning.

 Remove the cucumber from the bowl and drain off any surplus marinade. Spoon the minty cream cheese into a piping bag with a decorative nozzle and pipe a line of cheese in the center of each piece of cucumber.

 Arrange the cucumber on a serving dish and refrigerate until required.

TIME: *Preparation takes about 30 minutes, plus marinating.*

Aunt Ada's Potatoes

SERVES 4

This dish serves 4 as a vegetable accompaniment or 2 as a main course

INGREDIENTS
2 large baking potatoes, evenly sized
a little oil
2 egg yolks
4 ounces Red Leicester cheese, grated
salt and freshly ground black pepper
1 ounce salted peanuts
4 tablespoons fresh breadcrumbs
1 ounce grated Parmesan cheese
a little melted butter

Scrub the potatoes under cold running water and prick all over with a fork. Brush the potatoes with a little oil if desired; this will give them a shiny finish. Place the potatoes directly onto the shelf of a preheated oven at 425°F for approximately an hour or until the potato feels soft inside when gently squeezed.

Take a sharp knife and cut the baked potatoes in half. Scoop out the flesh into a mixing bowl, leaving a thin layer next to the skin.

Mash the potato and beat in the egg yolks one at a time, then stir in the Red Leicester cheese and season well.

Using the back of a knife lightly crush the peanuts and mix them with the breadcrumbs and grated Parmesan cheese. Pile the potato mixture back into the skins and sprinkle generously with the breadcrumb mixture.

Drizzle a little melted butter over the tops of the potatoes and return them to the oven for 15 minutes until they have heated through. Place under a preheated broiler for a few minutes prior to serving.

TIME: *Preparation takes about 20 minutes. Cooking takes approximately 1 hour 15 minutes.*

Cheese-stuffed Battered Mushrooms with Blueberry Sauce

SERVES 4

These mushrooms would be great as a starter or as part of a buffet

INGREDIENTS

12 medium cup mushrooms

8 ounces cream cheese

4 scallions, finely chopped

oil for deep frying

FOR THE BATTER

4 ounces all-purpose flour

pinch of salt

1 tablespoon olive oil

$^2/_3$ cup water

1 egg white

FOR THE SAUCE

8 ounces fresh blueberries

4 tablespoons superfine sugar

a little water

Make the batter first because fritter batter benefits greatly from standing for a while. Sift the flour and salt into a mixing bowl and make a well in the center. Pour in the olive oil and water and beat with a wooden spoon, gradually incorporating all the flour until you have a thick, smooth batter. Cover and leave for an hour. Just prior to using, stiffly beat the egg white and fold in.

To make the blueberry sauce, put all the ingredients in a saucepan and place over a low heat, stirring regularly, until the fruit has softened and the sauce has thickened and reduced a little. Keep warm until serving.

Carefully remove the stalks from the mushrooms and discard. Beat the cream cheese in a bowl until it becomes soft then add the scallions and continue beating for a minute or two.

Taking teaspoonfuls of the cream cheese mixture, stuff the mushroom caps generously and smooth over the surface.

Heat the oil for deep frying in a large saucepan. It has reached the correct temperature when traces of blue smoke begin to rise from the oil. Dip the mushrooms into the batter one at a time and let any excess batter run back into the bowl. Fry no more than 2 mushrooms at a time so you can keep an eye on their progress; they will take approximately 2–3 minutes to cook to a lovely golden brown.

Keep the cooked mushrooms hot until they are all fried, then serve accompanied by a sauceboat of blueberry sauce.

TIME: *Preparation takes about 20 minutes.*
Cooking takes approximately 25 minutes.

Individual Tomato Salads

SERVES 4

A *slice of Italian sunshine*

INGREDIENTS
4 ripe beef tomatoes
8 ounces mozzarella cheese, cubed
8 ounces black olives, pitted
1 red onion, thinly sliced
1 tablespoon chopped oregano leaves
olive oil and black pepper, to serve

FOR THE DRESSING
4 tablespoons olive oil
2 tablespoons white wine vinegar
salt and freshly ground black pepper

Cut the tops from the tomatoes and using a teaspoon, remove the insides and discard.
Place the next 4 ingredients in a bowl and lightly mix.
Put the dressing ingredients in a screw-top jar and shake thoroughly to mix. Pour over the filling, mix with the fingertips and season generously.
Spoon the filling into the tomato shells and spoon over any remaining dressing. Replace the lids.
Arrange the tomatoes on a serving dish, brush the outsides with a little olive oil and grind over lots of black pepper so that it sticks to the shells.

TIME: *Preparation takes about 30 minutes.*

Stuffed Baby Bell Peppers

SERVES 4

T*hese sweet-tasting peppers are a joy to cook with*

INGREDIENTS
8 red baby bell peppers
8-ounce carton plain cottage cheese
2 tablespoons snipped chives
salt and freshly ground black pepper
few frisée lettuce leaves, washed
3 tablespoons olive oil
12 pitted black olives, cut into rings
juice of 1 lemon

Remove stalks from the peppers and cut them in half lengthways. Carefully pull out the core and seeds and set the peppers to one side briefly.
Empty the cottage cheese into a mixing bowl and stir in the snipped chives and plenty of black pepper. Using a teaspoon fill the peppers with the cottage cheese mixture and arrange them on a serving platter lined with the washed lettuce leaves.
Place the olive oil, lemon juice and plenty of seasoning in a screw-top jar and shake vigorously to mix.
Pour the dressing over the stuffed peppers and scatter with the sliced olives. Keep refrigerated until required.

TIME: *Preparation takes about 30 minutes.*

Cheese Soufflé Potatoes

SERVES 4

Soufflés are not difficult to prepare and look very impressive when served

INGREDIENTS
4 large baking potatoes
2 tablespoons butter
2 tablespoons all-purpose flour
1¼ cups milk
salt and freshly ground black pepper
2 eggs, separated
4 ounces freshly grated Parmesan
freshly grated nutmeg

58

Scrub the potatoes under cold running water and prick all over with a fork.

Place the potatoes directly onto the shelf of a preheated oven at 425°F for about an hour or until the potato feels soft when gently squeezed. When the potatoes are cooked reduce the oven temperature to 400°F.

Melt the butter in a saucepan over a low heat and add the flour, stir the two together for a few minutes to allow the flour to cook. Slowly add the milk a little at a time to begin with then increase the flow, stirring all the time, until all the milk has been incorporated and the sauce is thick and smooth.

Cut a slice from the top of each potato and scoop out the soft potato flesh, leaving a thick wall against the skin. Mash the potato well and beat in the egg yolks and plenty of seasoning.

Add the thick sauce and grated Parmesan and continue beating until they are well combined. In a separate bowl whisk the egg whites until stiff and, using a metal spoon, carefully fold them into the sauce.

Spoon the soufflé mixture back into the potato shells and grate a little fresh nutmeg into each potato. Return the potatoes to the oven and continue cooking for a further 20 minutes until the soufflé is risen and browned. Serve immediately.

TIME: *Preparation takes about 35 minutes. Cooking takes approximately 1 hour 20 minutes.*

Baked Potatoes with Cauliflower & Almond Curry

SERVES 4

This spicy vegetarian curry goes very well with baked potatoes

INGREDIENTS
4 large baking potatoes, evenly sized

4 tablespoons butter

1 onion, thinly sliced

1 teaspoon ground turmeric

2 teaspoons ground cilantro

1 teaspoon ground cumin

1 small cauliflower

2 ounces blanched almonds, roughly chopped

2 ounces frozen peas, defrosted

2 ounces desiccated coconut

mango chutney, to serve

Scrub the potatoes under cold running water and prick with a fork.

Place directly onto the shelf of a preheated oven at 425°F for about an hour or until the potatoes feel soft when gently squeezed.

While they are cooking prepare the curry. Melt the butter in a skillet and fry the sliced onion until soft and golden brown.

Add the spices to the skillet and fry, stirring continuously for a few minutes.

Cut the cauliflower into small flowerets and add to the skillet along with the almonds and peas. Gently stir the vegetables so they become coated in spice then add sufficient cold water to moisten the curry and create a small amount of sauce.

Gently simmer the curry for about 10 minutes, adding a little extra water as and when necessary.

When all the vegetables are tender sprinkle over the coconut and stir it into the curry. Continue cooking for a few more minutes then remove the skillet from the heat.

When the potatoes have finished baking, split them in half and scoop out some of the cooked insides. Roughly chop half of the potato flesh and add it to the curry.

Reheat the curry briefly and share it among the potatoes. Serve immediately accompanied by mango chutney.

TIME: *Preparation takes about 20 minutes. Cooking takes approximately 1 hour.*

59

Globe Artichoke with Hollandaise Sauce

SERVES 4

The *globe artichoke is a tasty but often overlooked vegetable*

INGREDIENTS
4 medium globe artichokes
2 teaspoons lemon juice
salt and freshly ground black pepper
3 egg yolks
1 cup cold butter
fresh nutmeg

Cut the stalk off the artichokes as close to the base of the vegetable as possible. Remove any discolored outer leaves since they are likely to be tough, and snip off the tips of the remaining leaves with a sharp pair of scissors.

Add a few drops of lemon juice to a saucepan of salted water, bring to a boil and drop in the prepared artichokes. Cover and leave to simmer gently for approximately 40 minutes.

The sauce is very simple to make but must not be hurried or the eggs will cook too much and scramble. Place the egg yolks and 2 teaspoons of lemon juice in a heat-resistant bowl, season well and stand over a saucepan of gently bubbling water.

Using a balloon whisk, whisk the mixture for a few minutes until it thickens a little. Remove the butter from the refrigerator and chop it into pieces not much bigger than a pea. Feed these slowly into the egg yolks, one at a time, making sure that each is incorporated into the sauce before another is added.

Slowly the sauce will thicken and when complete will have the look and consistency of fresh mayonnaise. Because the sauce never gets hot during cooking, it should be kept at similarly low temperatures until served. This is best achieved by standing the bowl of sauce in warm water.

When the artichokes are tender, remove them from the water and drain briefly upside down on paper towel. When well drained use a teaspoon to gently scrape away and remove the choke from the center of the vegetable.

Place the artichokes on a serving dish and spoon the Hollandaise sauce into the center of each. Grate over a little fresh nutmeg and serve immediately.

TIME: *Preparation takes about 30 minutes. Cooking takes approximately 45 minutes.*

Mushrooms with Pine Nuts & Tapenade

SERVES 4

A *simple starter or snack full of Mediterranean flavors*

INGREDIENTS
8 large flat cap mushrooms
4 tablespoons tapenade (olive paste)
2 tablespoons pine nuts
2 tablespoons fresh breadcrumbs
salt and freshly ground black pepper
olive oil

▌ Wipe the mushroom caps and cut off as much of the stalk as possible. Place gills upward on a lightly oiled baking sheet.
▌ Divide the tapenade among the mushrooms and gently spread it out to cover the gills completely.
▌ Crush the pine nuts using a pestle and mortar or the heel of a knife and sprinkle them over the tapenade. Top with a layer of breadcrumbs and a little seasoning.
▌ Drizzle a little olive oil over the mushrooms and place under a preheated broiler for 5–10 minutes until the top of the stuffing has browned and the mushrooms are tender.

TIME: *Preparation takes about 15 minutes. Cooking takes approximately 10 minutes.*

Rice-stuffed Peppers

SERVES 4

The *pesto livens up the rice filling*

INGREDIENTS
4 squat green bell peppers
olive oil
salt and freshly ground black pepper

FOR THE FILLING
12 ounces cooked long grain and wild rice mixture
2 ounces roughly chopped walnuts
1 tablespoon slivered almonds, toasted
2 tablespoons green pesto
4 ounces dried prunes, stoned and chopped

▌ Cut the tops from the peppers and remove the seeds and core. Place the peppers and lids in a large bowl and pour over sufficient boiling water to cover them. Allow to stand for 5 minutes then pour off the water and drain the pepper shells upside-down on paper towel.
▌ Mix together all the filling ingredients. Season well and pack into the pepper shells.
▌ Place on a baking sheet, cover with the pepper tops and lightly brush with a little olive oil. Grind over some black pepper and place them in a preheated oven at 350°F for 40 minutes.

TIME: *Preparation takes about 20 minutes. Cooking takes approximately 1 hour.*

62

Stir-fried Vegetables on Eggplant Rafts

SERVES 4

Stir-frying baby vegetables keeps all the fresh flavors intact

INGREDIENTS

2 medium eggplants

salt

4 tablespoons olive oil

2 tablespoons peanut oil

1 bunch scallions, sliced diagonally

1 pound mixed baby vegetables such as
corn, carrots, French beans, button mushrooms

2 ounces unsalted peanuts

2 tablespoons sesame seeds

1 tablespoon light soy sauce

▍Cut each eggplant lengthways into 4 thick slices, lay on a baking sheet and sprinkle liberally with salt.

▍Leave the eggplants for 30 minutes to extract the bitter juices then rinse off under cold running water and pat dry.

▍Reserve the 2 inner slices from each eggplant for frying; 2 outer slices should be chopped to roughly the same size as the baby vegetables.

▍Heat 2 tablespoons of the olive oil in a skillet and fry 2 of the eggplant slices until tender and lightly browned. Place them in a medium oven to keep hot while you repeat the process with the remaining olive oil and the other 2 slices. Keep hot while you stir-fry the vegetables.

▍Heat the peanut oil in a wok or high-sided skillet and fry the scallions for approximately 3 minutes.

▍Add the baby vegetables and chopped eggplant to the pan and continue cooking for a further 3 minutes until they are cooked but still crisp.

▍Add the peanuts and sesame seeds and fry for another minute then add the soy sauce and heat through briefly.

▍Remove the fried eggplant slices from the oven, transfer them to their serving dishes and spoon the stir-fried vegetables over the top. Serve immediately.

TIME: *Preparation takes about 10 minutes.*
Cooking takes approximately 20 minutes.

Multicolored Roast Peppers with Ratatouille

SERVES 6

It *is hard to imagine a more colorful dish*

INGREDIENTS
1 large eggplant, thickly sliced
salt and freshly ground black pepper
6 large bell peppers, as many different
colors as possible
olive oil
2 medium onions, thinly sliced
4 cloves garlic, roughly chopped
4 zucchinis, thinly sliced
2 teaspoons dried thyme
stalk of fresh rosemary
2x14-ounce cans chopped tomatoes
1 tablespoon tomato paste
fresh chopped parsley (for garnish)
freshly grated Parmesan cheese

Spread the eggplant slices over a baking sheet and sprinkle generously with salt, set aside for 30 minutes to extract the bitter juices.

Cut all the peppers in half lengthways through the stalk and remove the core and seeds.

Arrange the peppers on a baking sheet, brush with a little olive oil and grind over plenty of black pepper. Set aside briefly.

Heat 4 tablespoons of olive oil in a large saucepan and fry the sliced onion and garlic until soft and golden brown. Rinse off the eggplant slices and add to the pan along with the zucchinis. Fry for a couple of minutes so they can absorb the garlic-flavored oil.

Add the dried thyme and fresh rosemary and fry for a few seconds before adding the canned tomatoes and tomato paste.

Season well and leave to simmer, uncovered, over a low heat until the sauce thickens and the vegetables are cooked but retain their shape.

While the ratatouille is cooking place the baking sheet of peppers into a preheated oven at 350°F and cook until they soften and the skins catch slightly. Cooking peppers this way intensifies the already bright colors of the flesh and they look stunning.

This dish looks most impressive brought to the table on a large round or oval serving plate. Carefully arrange the roasted peppers around the edge of the dish in alternating colors with the stalks facing outward.

Fish out the rosemary stalk and ladle spoonfuls of the ratatouille over the peppers, leaving the stalk end exposed.

Grate over lots of black pepper and scatter over handfuls of roughly chopped parsley.

Serve right away with a bowl of freshly grated Parmesan cheese for sprinkling.

TIME: *Preparation takes about 30 minutes, plus standing.*
Cooking takes approximately 45 minutes.

65

Mushrooms on Mushrooms

SERVES 4

For real mushroom addicts!

INGREDIENTS
2 ounces dried Ceps
8 large flat mushrooms
2 tablespoons olive oil
2 ounces Oyster mushrooms
4 ounces Shiitake mushrooms
3 cloves garlic, chopped
1 tablespoon pine nuts
4 tablespoons grated Parmesan cheese
freshly ground black pepper
chopped parsley, to garnish

Place the dried Ceps in a small amount of tepid water for 20 minutes to reconstitute.

Wipe the caps of the large flat mushrooms and cut off the stalk. Place gills upward on a baking sheet brushed with a little olive oil.

When the Ceps are ready, drain the water from them and roughly chop them with the Oyster and Shiitake mushrooms.

Heat the olive oil in a skillet and fry the chopped garlic until brown.

Add the chopped mushrooms to the skillet and fry, tossing them in the oil until they have absorbed the oil and garlic flavor. Add the pine nuts to the skillet and stir to coat them in the oil.

Spoon the topping onto the large mushroom caps and pour over any surplus cooking liquor. Cover loosely with tinfoil and place in a preheated oven at 350°F for 15 minutes until the large mushrooms are just tender.

Remove the tinfoil and share the grated Parmesan among the mushrooms. Grind some black pepper over each one and place under a preheated broiler until the cheese melts and turns golden brown.

Generously garnish with chopped parsley and transfer to serving dishes. Serve with plenty of fresh bread to soak up the juices.

TIME: *Preparation takes about 10 minutes, plus soaking.*
Cooking takes approximately 30 minutes.

Blue Vinney Parsnip Peppers

SERVES 4

This recipe brings a new dimension to stuffed peppers

INGREDIENTS

8 ounces parsnips

4 squat yellow bell peppers, evenly sized

4 tablespoons butter

4 tablespoons all-purpose flour

1 1/4 cups fresh milk

6 ounces Blue Vinney cheese (or Blue Stilton)

2 ounces walnut pieces

1 ounce raisins

salt and freshly ground black pepper

4 teaspoons green pesto

Peel the parsnips and cut them into even-sized pieces of roughly 3/4-inch square. Blanch in boiling water for about 5 minutes then drain and set aside on paper towel until required.

Cut the tops from the peppers, remove the seeds and place in a large bowl with their tops. Pour over sufficient boiling water to cover, leave to stand for about 5 minutes then drain off the water.

Melt the butter in a saucepan over a low heat, add the flour and stir for a couple of minutes to allow the flour to cook. Gradually add the milk to the pan, stirring all the time, until you have a thick, smooth sauce.

Remove the rind from the cheese and discard. Chop the cheese into small pieces and stir into the sauce along with the walnut pieces, raisins and blanched parsnip. Gently stir the sauce to combine the ingredients and finish with plenty of seasoning.

Spread a teaspoon of pesto over the inside of each pepper and fill to the brim with spoonfuls of the cheese and parsnip sauce. Push out the green stalk from the tops of the peppers and place one on top of each pepper to make a lid.

Place in a preheated oven at 325°F for 35–40 minutes until the flesh of the peppers is tender and the tops are just beginning to brown. Serve immediately.

TIME: *Preparation takes about 15 minutes. Cooking takes approximately 1 hour.*

69

Eggplant Provençale

SERVES 4

This is an all-in-one vegetable dish

INGREDIENTS

2 large eggplants
6 tablespoons olive oil
1 large onion, thinly sliced
2 cloves garlic, roughly chopped
1 red bell pepper, seeded and chopped
2 zucchinis, thinly sliced
stalk of fresh rosemary
1 bay leaf
14-ounce can chopped tomatoes
²/₃ cup red wine
salt and freshly ground black pepper
4 tablespoons Parmesan cheese, grated

Cut the eggplants in half lengthways and sprinkle the cut surface with salt. Allow to stand for 30 minutes to extract the bitter juices then rinse off the salt and pat dry.

While the eggplant is standing, begin preparing the filling. Heat 4 tablespoons of olive oil in a large saucepan and fry the onion and garlic until lightly browned.

Add the pepper and zucchinis to the pan and continue frying for a couple of minutes until they begin to soften.

Drop the stalk of rosemary and the bay leaf into the pan. Stir into the vegetables briefly then add the chopped tomatoes and red wine. Season well and leave on a low heat to simmer gently for about 20 minutes.

Heat the remaining olive oil in a skillet and fry the eggplant halves for a couple of minutes on each side. Lift out of the pan when cooked and drain them on paper towel. Set aside to cool.

Scoop out the cooled eggplant flesh with a spoon, leaving a thin layer next to the skin. Roughly chop the eggplant and add it to the vegetables.

The filling is ready when the vegetables are cooked but still retain their shape and the sauce is thick and glossy. Remove the rosemary and bay leaf and correct the seasoning.

Arrange the eggplant "shells" on a baking sheet and spoon generous quantities of filling into each one. Sprinkle with grated Parmesan.

Place in a preheated oven at 400°F for 10 minutes to heat through thoroughly and melt the cheese into a crust.

TIME: *Preparation takes about 30 minutes, plus standing.*
Cooking takes approximately 50 minutes.

70

Oh So Garlicky Peppers

SERVES 4

This recipe is one for real lovers of garlic

INGREDIENTS
8 baby bell peppers
8 cloves garlic, peeled
salt and freshly ground black pepper
olive oil
4 shallots, very finely chopped
1 red chili, seeded and chopped
4 ounces pitted black olives, finely chopped
fresh breadcrumbs

Cut the tops from the peppers and carefully remove the seeds and core. Rub the inside of each pepper with a clove of garlic and set to one side.

To make the garlic into a paste suitable for frying, place the cloves on a nonabsorbent work surface and sprinkle with a little salt. Begin chopping them with the heel of a large knife. As the garlic is chopped the salt will draw the moisture from inside the cloves and you will soon have a useable paste.

Heat 2 tablespoons of olive oil in a small skillet and fry the shallots and chopped chili until they are soft. Try not to let the shallots brown. Add the garlic paste and continue frying for a minute, then add the chopped olives and fry for a further minute.

Season well, then begin adding breadcrumbs a tablespoon at a time, stirring continually, until you have sufficient stuffing for the peppers.

Remove the pan from the heat and using a teaspoon, pack the garlic stuffing into the baby peppers. Place the lids on top and lightly brush the outsides of the peppers with a little olive oil, grind some black pepper over and arrange the peppers on a baking sheet.

Place in a preheated oven at 350°F and cook for approximately 15–20 minutes or until the flesh is tender.

When cooked, transfer the peppers to a serving dish and serve either as a starter or as a vegetable accompaniment to a main course.

TIME: *Preparation takes about 25 minutes. Cooking takes approximately 40 minutes.*

Plum Tomatoes with Horseradish & Watercress Pasta

SERVES 4

Sweet-tasting plum tomatoes contrast sharply with this mayonnaise

INGREDIENTS
salt and freshly ground black pepper
8 ounces small pasta (e.g. conchiglie or piccole)
olive oil
4 large plum tomatoes, slightly under-ripe
3 tablespoons fresh mayonnaise (see page 11)
2 teaspoons cream of horseradish sauce
1 ounce raisins
1 bunch watercress

Bring a saucepan of lightly salted water to a boil and drop in the pasta with a little olive oil to prevent sticking. Cook the pasta until just tender (al dente), then drain off the cooking water.

Toss the cooked pasta in a sprinkling of olive oil and set aside to cool.

Cut the plum tomatoes in half lengthways and using a teaspoon scoop out the insides and discard, taking care not to damage the skins. Set aside.

Place the mayonnaise in a bowl and beat in the horseradish sauce and raisins. Season well.

Discard any rough-looking watercress and wash the remainder in plenty of cold water. Drain and shake thoroughly to remove as much water as possible then cut off most of the stalks. Finely chop the remaining watercress to a fine pulp and stir into the mayonnaise.

Stir the mayonnaise into the cooled pasta, adding a small amount at a time. Add just enough to bind the pasta together and create a little surplus sauce. If there is any mayonnaise left over it is better to refrigerate it for future use than use too much.

Spoon generous quantities of the pasta salad into the tomato shells and transfer them to serving dishes. Serve with brown bread and butter and the pepper mill.

TIME: *Preparation takes about 30 minutes. Cooking takes approximately 5 minutes.*

Leeky Potatoes

Lightly fried leeks and a good cheese sauce were made for each other

INGREDIENTS

4 large baking potatoes

2 medium leeks

2 tablespoons butter

2 tablespoons flour

1¼ cups fresh milk

2 tablespoons olive oil

4 ounces strong cheddar cheese, grated

1 egg yolk

salt and freshly ground black pepper

Scrub the potatoes under cold running water and prick all over with a fork. Place them directly onto the shelf of a preheated oven at 425°F for approximately 1 hour or until the potato feels soft when gently squeezed.

While the potatoes are baking prepare the filling. Make a deep cut into each leek roughly three-quarters of its length and wash the insides thoroughly to remove any soil. Set to one side to drain.

To make the cheese sauce, melt the butter over a low heat, add the flour and stir the two together for a couple of minutes to allow the flour to cook.

Slowly add the milk a little at a time to begin with, stirring continuously, then increase the flow until all the milk is used and you have a thick, smooth sauce.

Stir in 2 ounces of the grated Cheddar cheese and plenty of seasoning. Set the sauce to one side.

Cut the cleaned leeks in half and slice each one into ¾-inch lengths.

Heat the olive oil in a skillet and fry the leeks for a couple of minutes until they are softened but not browned. Stir the cooked leeks into the cheese sauce.

When the potatoes are cooked, slice a lid from the top of each one and scoop out the soft flesh using a teaspoon, leaving a good layer of potato next to the skin.

Mash half of the potato innards with the egg yolk, the remaining grated cheese and freshly ground black pepper, and share equally among the potato shells.

Fill the potatoes to the top with the cheese and leek mixture and cover with the lids. Return to the oven for 10 minutes to heat through and serve immediately.

TIME: *Preparation takes about 25 minutes. Cooking takes approximately 1 hour 10 minutes.*

Onion & Goats' Cheese

SERVES 4

Goats' cheese is the essence of France

INGREDIENTS
2 medium red onions
olive oil
12 ounces goats' cheese
2 ounces pine nuts
handful of fresh basil leaves

Place the unpeeled onions onto the shelf of a preheated oven at 400°F for 20 minutes.

Carefully remove the skin from the part-cooked onions and cut them in half through the root end. Remove a few of the inner layers of onion to create an onion bowl, brush with a little olive oil and place on a baking sheet.

Chop the goats' cheese into small pieces and place in a bowl with the pine nuts. Bruise the basil with the handle of a knife to release the flavor, then tear into the bowl.

Brush a little olive oil onto the fingertips and lightly mix the stuffing ingredients together. Place handfuls in the onion bowls. Do not overfill. Store any leftover stuffing in the refrigerator.

Reduce the oven temperature to 350°F and return the stuffed onions to the oven for 10–15 minutes or until the cheese has softened.

Serve with plenty of cheese biscuits and French bread and perhaps a glass or two of port.

TIME: *Preparation takes about 25 minutes.*
Cooking takes approximately 35 minutes.

Artichoke Hearts with Tapenade

SERVES 4

The Italian artichoke and the French tapenade combine beautifully

INGREDIENTS
2 cans large artichoke hearts
4 tablespoons tapenade (olive paste)
2 egg yolks, lightly beaten
fresh breadcrumbs for coating
salt and freshly ground black pepper
oil for deep frying
tomato sauce for dipping

75

Remove artichokes from the cans and drain thoroughly. If possible choose larger artichokes for this recipe since they are easier to prepare and look better when served.

Cut the hearts in half from top to bottom and remove one or two of the layers from the middle of each half. Spoon a little tapenade into each cavity.

Dip the stuffed artichokes into the beaten egg yolk and roll in breadcrumbs seasoned with a little salt and pepper. Heat the oil in a deep-fat fryer and cook 2 or 3 at a time until golden.

Lift the cooked artichokes from the oil on a slotted spoon and transfer to paper towel.

When they are all cooked transfer to a suitable dish and serve immediately with tomato sauce.

TIME: *Preparation takes about 20 minutes.*
Cooking takes approximately 15 minutes.

Index